How to Make Money on Craigslist

Contents

1. What is Craigslist?

The History of Craigslist

The popular website, Craigslist.com, was created by Craig Newmark in 1995 as an email distribution list of friends, featuring local events in the San Francisco Bay Area, before becoming a web-based service in 1996. It was incorporated as a private, for-profit company in 1999 and has been expanding to cover more and more different cities since then.

Craigslist founder Craig Newmark observed people helping one another in friendly, social and trusting communal ways on the Internet via the WELL, MindVox and Usenet, and felt isolated as a relative newcomer to San Francisco. He decided to create something similar for local events.

The first emailed San Francisco event listings debuted in early 1995. The initial technology encountered some limits, so by June 1995 new software was installed to handle the expanding website better and the mailing list "Craigslist" resumed operations. Newmark submitted most of the early posting himself and they were notices of social events of interest to software and Internet developers living and working in the San Francisco Bay area.

Soon, word-of-mouth led to rapid growth. The number of subscribers and postings grew rapidly. There was no moderation and Newmark was surprised when people started using the mailing list for non-event postings. People trying to get technical positions filled found that the list was a good way to reach people with the skills they were looking for.

This led to the addition of a category for jobs. User demand for more categories resulted in the list of categories growing and expanding.

Community members started asking for a web interface. Newmark enlisted the help of volunteers and contractors to create a website user interface for the different mailing list categories.

In need of a domain name for this, Craig registered Craigslist.org (as well as Craigslist.com later on, to prevent the name from being used for other purposes). Around the time of these events, Newmark realized that the site was growing so fast that he could stop working as a software engineer and work full time running Craigslist. By April 2000, there were nine employees working out of Newmark's apartment on Cole Street in San Francisco.

Newmark says that Craigslist works because it gives people a voice, a sense of community trust and even intimacy. Other factors he cites are consistency of down-to-earth values, customer service and simplicity. Newmark was approached with an offer for running banner ads on Craigslist, but he decided to decline. In 2002, Craigslist staff posted mock-banner ads throughout the site as an April Fools joke.

In 2001, the company started the Craigslist Foundation, a section 501(c) nonprofit organization that connects people to the resources they need to strengthen communities and neighborhoods. It offers free and low-cost events and online resources to promote community building at all levels. It accepts charitable donations and, rather than directly funding organizations, it produces "Face-to-face events and offers online resources to help grassroots organizations get off the ground and contribute real value to the community."

Since 2004, the Craigslist Foundation has hosted an annual conference called Boot Camp, an in-person event that focuses on skills for connecting, motivating and inspiring greater community involvement and impact. Boot

Camp has drawn more than 10,000 passionate people since its inception. The next Boot Camp event will be held on Saturday, August 14, 2010.

The Craigslist Foundation is also the fiscal sponsor for Our Good Works, the organization that manages AllforGood.org, an application that distributes volunteer opportunities across the web and helps people get involved in their communities.

Craigslist Today

As of 2009 Craigslist.com has a staff of 28 people and makes most of its money from paid job ads in cities like San Francisco, New York City, Los Angeles, San Diego, Boston, Seattle, Washington D.C., Chicago, Philadelphia and Portland, Oregon – and paid broker apartment listings in New York City.

The site serves over twenty billion page views per month, putting it in 33rd place overall among web sites worldwide and 7th place overall among web sites in the United States, with over 49.4 million unique monthly visitors in the United States alone .

With over eighty million new classified advertisements each month, Craigslist is the leading classifieds service in any medium. The site receives over two million new job listings each month, making it one of the top job boards in the world. The classified advertisements range from traditional buy/sell ads and community announcements to personal ads and erotic ads.

One of the most notable things about Craigslist.com is that it has gone through very little aesthetic changes since 1996 and even for that time it's extremely simple and basic.

Today there are a plethora of options for users to choose from as far as which types of listings can be searched though or posted. Craigslist has comprehensive for-sale listings with everything from cars to household appliances. The website also has an extensive jobs/services section as well as a classifieds section for social interaction.

You can sell just about anything on Craigslist. People post ads for everyday items, brand new items sold in bulk or used collectables. Craigslist is renowned for being one of the primary online sources of local, affordable merchandise.

Selling digital content is also possible on Craigslist, usually with the help of a third-party website service for processing funds and delivering content. In this respect Craigslist works as an excellent advertising system wherein every poster gets at least a few minutes at the "top of the list" sweet spot.

Lastly there are untold profits to be made by seeking jobs on Craigslist or offering services. Craigslist has both employer-seeking ads as well as employee-seeking ads. You can provide service to local people and get paid per-job like a contractor, you can find local full-time and part-time jobs or you can look for someone to do the work for you.

As you can see there are nearly limitless opportunities to make profit from Craigslist.com. It's one of the most diverse websites for buying/selling goods and services and it's completely free! All you need to do to start profiting from Craigslist is figure out what you want to do (Sell junk, offer your services or provide digital content) and figure out how to use the website!

2. How Do I Use Craigslist?

Getting Started

Using Craigslist is easy, and navigating the site is fairly straight-forward. The first thing you'll want to do is create an account. Start by finding your local Craigslist page. Each major city (and sometimes county or area) has its own page on which listings are specific to that respective metro area. You can choose from the list of major cities on the Craigslist homepage, or click into your state and your local market from there.

From there just look at the panel on the left-hand side of the screen. Select "Login" or "My Account" and you'll be directed to the sign-in page. Directly under the yellow box where a preexisting user would sign in there's a link that says "Sign up for an account." Signing up is not mandatory but if you're serious about using Craigslist for making money then you're going to want to create an account.

I recommend using a secondary e-mail as your Craigslist e-mail. It's not uncommon to receive spam e-mails or unwanted e-mails mixed in with legitimate e-mails on Craigslist, especially if your postings become popular or contain main mainstream key-words. It's best to get a free e-mail account with a reputable e-mail website like www.yahoo.com or www.gmail.com and have that account be only for your Craigslist-related e-mail traffic.

Another great option for Yahoo! E-mail users is to create a folder especially for Craigslist posting e-mails. First you have to create a new folder by selecting "Add" which is located right above all your extra e-mail folders. After you've created the folder you then go to your Options and select Filters. In the filter you can just make a simple filter that redirects all e-mail with "Craigslist" in the sender's email address directly to that folder. This is convenient because it allows you to keep your Yahoo! E-mail address without having to worry about any clutter or disorganization from receiving lots of Craigslist-related e-mails.

If you like you can even create a Craigslist-related account and have it forwarded to your Yahoo! E-mail account. This is a great option because it allows you to have all of your e-mails saved on two different e-mail accounts for back up purposes. G-mail is the best option for this.

You can forward your G-mail e-mail to your Yahoo! E-mail inbox and then have those e-mails filtered so that they go into your Craigslist folder. You can further add functionality to this set up by linking your G-mail account with your Yahoo! Account so that you can send e-mails from your Yahoo! Account "as" your G-mail account (e.g. Your Yahoo! Account is bizznissman@yahoo.com and your G-mail account is bizznizz_Craigslist@G-mail.com. You can send e-mails from bizznizz_Craigslist@gmail.com while on your Yahoo! E-mail account.) Yahoo's free e-mail service allows you to link 1 other e-mail account in this way (The paid version allows more).

Forwarding your G-mail:

Click Settings at the top of any Gmail page, and open the Forwarding and POP/IMAP tab.

1. From the first drop-down menu in the Forwarding section, select 'Add new email address.'
2. Enter the email address to which you'd like your messages forwarded.
3. For your security, we'll send verification to that email address.
4. Open your forwarding email account, and find the confirmation message from the Gmail team.
5. Click the verification link in that email.

6. Back in your Gmail account, select the 'Forward a copy of incoming mail to...' option and select your forwarding address from the drop-down menu.
7. Select the action you'd like your messages to take from the drop-down menu. You can choose to keep Gmail's copy of the message in your inbox, or you can send it automatically to All Mail or Trash.
8. Click Save Changes.

Linking Yahoo! and G-mail accounts:

1. Sign in to the Yahoo! Mail account into which you want to access the external account.
2. In the upper-right corner of the Mail page, click the Options link, then select Mail Options from the menu. Click the Options link, then select Mail Options.
3. Click the Accounts link on the left. Click the Accounts link.
4. To set up the account to send email from Yahoo! Mail:
    1) In the Sending Mail section of the page, enter a name for the new account (for example, Work or School). Type a name for the new account.
    2) Next enter a "From" name and the email address of the non-Yahoo! email account. Specify a From name and the email address for the external account.
    3) When someone replies to a message that you send from the non-Yahoo! account, the reply automatically goes back to the email address associated with the account. If you want, you can specify a different default reply-to address, such as your Yahoo! Mail address, for responses to be sent to.
    4) Click the Change reply-to address link next to the Email address.
    5) Click the Change reply-to address link.
    6) A Reply-to address box opens

7)   Enter the reply-to address you want to use instead of the account's email address.

8)   Enter a reply-to address.

9)   4. If you plan to use Yahoo! Mail only to send messages from this account , you're done. Click the Save Changes button to finish adding the new account. Click Save Changes

10)   The Verify Email Address window opens. You must verify that you are the owner of the non-Yahoo! account before you can send email from it. See below for more on how to verify the account.

After you've got your e-mails and your Craigslist account set up you're free to start posting ads or searching for them. Here's a brief explanation of each category and subcategory in Craigslist:

1) Community

    a) Community based listings

    b) Carpooling, classes, volunteer work etc.

    c) This section is basically a community information board.

2) Personals

    a) Friendship and Romance personals

3) Discussion Forums

    a) Basic online forum with many different topics.

4) Housing

    a) Basic apartment/house searching section.

    b) Find roommates or places to live.

    c) Rent out or sell your own property.

5) For Sale

    a) Most active section on Craigslist.

    b) Sell your junk or online content here.

    c) You can also post "Looking for" ads to try and attract sellers of a particular product.

6) Gigs

    a) Very similar to the jobs section but made especially for freelance positions.

    b) Contains freelance jobs, musical gigs and temp work.

    c) Offer your freelance services such as TV Repair or Computer Maintenance.

7) Jobs

    a) Primary service/job seeking area.

    b) Look for jobs in many different areas from media to real estate.

    c) Offer your services and post your information.

Searching for Ads

To look for a particular listing just click on one of the subcategories. You'll be taken to a page that has the most recent listings for that category as well as the search interface.

The search interface is pretty self-explanatory. Just enter the search term and press the search button. You can select a specific subcategory from the drop down box and decide if you want to view only posts that have images or any posts. If you're on a buying/selling category then you can set your minimum and maximum price. Lastly you can select "title only" or "entire post." This will determine how your search is carried out.

If you search for title only then the search engine will ignore any text within the posts and only look for your search phrase in the titles of posts. If you select entire post then the search engine will look though every post's content as well as the title and return any posts that have matching elements to your search phrase. Using title only is useful when you have a very specific item you're trying to find. Some posters also put loads of unrelated keywords in their posts to try and attract more traffic; selecting title only will prevent you from stumbling on one of these unrelated posts.

Posting your Ads

After you've created an account and logged in, you can post an ad easily by going to the appropriate category where you'd like to post the ad. In the top right corner of the screen there is a link labeled "[post]." Click the link and you'll be taken to a page where you can select the exact category that you'd like to post in.

Select the category and you'll be taken to the post creation screen. Here you'll be able to give your post a title and provide the information for the body of the post. If you're selling an item you will have the option to set the price and the specific location.

Here you'll have to input the e-mail address that you'd like replies to this ad to go to. You can have your e-mail published or you can select "anonymize." This will provide viewers with a randomly generated e-mail address by Craigslist to send e-mails to which will be forwarded to your actual e-mail address.

It is advised to always select anonymize to avoid having your e-mail publicly posted and therefore accessible by e-mail spam bots that will store that address in a database and send you constant spam from various sources.

After you've given your post a title and explained what your post is about, you'll have the option to add or edit images (Depending on the type of post you're making). Generally speaking it's smart to always ad images to your post regardless of what you're posting because many people will use the "has an image" feature while searching to weed out any posts where they can't see a product they're trying to buy etc

Once you select continue you'll be taken to a screen where you can see what your ad will look like once it's posted to Craigslist. If you're okay with your ad then select continue (Edit will take you to the previous page where you can make adjustments to your ad). You'll be taken to the Terms of Use page where you must agree in order to be able to post your ad. As with any Terms of Use contract it's important to read it thoroughly to ensure that you really want to abide to all the terms.

If you didn't create an account, here's where you will have to. You'll enter your e-mail and type the characters of a captcha code. If you did create an account just follow the remaining instructions and your ad will be posted.

After posting an ad Craigslist will send you an automated e-mail with a link to your ad and information on how to modify or delete it. Generally speaking it takes anywhere from 30 minutes to 24 hours for your posts to truly become public. Don't be discouraged if you can't find your post by searching for the appropriate terms. Just because you can't find your own ad does not mean that other people won't be able to see it.

Tips on Ad Writing

It's important to format your ads so that they're easy to read and brief. One of the biggest mistakes that new Craigslist posters make is that they provide too much information and their ads look like mini-novels.

People don't prefer to read large chunks of convoluted text. It's best to be concise and describe exactly what you're selling, providing or looking for in as few words as possible. The more eloquent you are the more likely someone is to actually read your ad instead of just skipping it over.

If you're selling an item you should always include the price in the title. Even though there's a price option, people generally don't take it seriously. Too many posters write down $1 or 2$ when they're actually selling much more expensive items. This makes searching by price somewhat inaccurate and unreliable. By including the price in your title you allow people to search by only title and be able to see the price of your item easily.

Don't post your personal information like e-mail, address or phone number in the body of your ads. Aside from being unsafe, this is a good way to get lots of spam. You can receive spam messages via snail mail, e-mail and even cell phone text messages!

If you're selling anything it's practically mandatory that you include an image of what you're selling. Including an image will dramatically increase your success rate as many people don't even look at posts that don't have images. Even if you don't have a picture of your product you can usually find an image by searching for it on an online market website like www.amazon.com or a search engine like www.google.com. Be careful though, using images from other sites may or may not be breaking copyright law, always try to ask for permission if possible or get images from public domain sources.

Another good tip is to provide comparative information in your post. If you're selling a computer at a competitive price then give a link to a different online market selling that monitor so that people can compare. If you sell a car you can link to its Kelly Blue Book page so people can see that they're getting a fair deal on the price.

Some items take time to sell. I recommend making a post for them every 2 to 3 weeks. Every post lasts for 30 days but the longer time goes by the less likely that anyone will look at your post. It's important not to make repeated posts every day, however, as this is against the terms of use and is considered spam.

General Writing Tips & Using Copy for Advertising

Part of being a successful Craigslist poster is being a decent writer. While it's not entirely necessary to have excellent writing skills, the better you are at conveying information the more likely people will be convinced to buy your product or hire you after they've read your listings.

Proper spelling and grammar is a first good step. It's important that people can understand what you're saying and a misplaced comma or inappropriately used semicolon can make people question your listings. Often times people become suspicious if an ad seems to have irregular punctuation because it seems like a possible way of disguising ulterior motive in the ad. For instance, you ad could read: Selling '91 Honda Accord, in "Good" condition. Does that mean the car is in *good* condition or does it mean the car is actually in bad condition and you're being facetious? Putting quotes around a word is <u>not</u> an acceptable way to show emphasis. Putting quotes around a word implies that it is either a direct quote from someone or that the word was used sarcastically.

Example A: According to Jim it's a "Very good" car.

In that example a man named Jim literally used the phrase "Very good" and the author quoted him.

Example B: Mary is really "helpful," if you know what I mean.

In that example the author is implying that Mary is not, in fact, very helpful at all. The author is using the phrase sarcastically.

Aside from grammar, eloquence and formatting are extremely important. As I said previously, you should be short and concise. When it comes to selling things on Craigslist people simply want to have the essential information. Craigslist is a fast-paced environment; people don't generally browse the website unless their ready or near-ready to purchase. Brevity is the key to a successful ad.

After you type your ad, go back and take note of how long it is. Are their any parts that you can sum up in fewer words? For example, your ad might say, "I'm selling my Workstation Computer. It has served me well over the past few years but I'm upgrading so I'm selling this to buy parts for my new computer. It works great; I haven't had any problems with it. It has 3GB of RAM, an Intel Processor and a 160GB Hard Drive."

That's a terrible way to start an ad. Quite frankly people don't really care why you're selling your item or what you're going to do with the money. Reading about it won't hurt the sale but the potential customer might never even read the ad if he or she sees how long it is. Instead you could have just said, "For Sale: Workstation Computer. 3GB of RAM, Intel Processor and 160GB Hard Drive. Works Great!"

Of course this all depends on who your target market is and exactly what you're selling. Sometimes it actually can benefit you to give the potential client or customer background information. In particular, if you're selling a used product that doesn't function 100% or has moderate to sever aesthetic damage then you might want to try and reassure the potential buyer with nonessential information. If you're selling a bike with a broken gear shifter, it might be beneficial to focus your ad on how well the bike served you in the past. This is a bit of marketing trickery.

At no point should you try to swindle customers into buying bad products, but there's no need to disclose 100% of the details in the initial sales ad. Get the customer interested with your Craigslist ad so they're willing to come see the product. This will greatly increase their chances of purchasing the product and forgiving its flaws. If you tell them about the busted gear shifter in the sales ad, they may not even contact you. If you tell them about it after they come to see it, there's a slight chance they'll buy the bike anyway out of convenience (most people don't want to have the feeling of driving somewhere for nothing).

Another good marketing tool is the shining example. You see this in commercials and magazines all the time, usually in the form of a celebrity endorsement. If you're selling an item that was endorsed by a celebrity or person of interest, by all means include that information in the description. As long as what you claim is 100% true and can be verified by reputable sources, it's perfectly legal to mention that an item or service was used by someone else. Did The Eagles use the exact same brand of guitar pick as the one you're selling? Then you're ad could read "Buy the Brand the Eagles Used!" Assuming you can prove that, at any point in time, the eagles really did use that exact brand of guitar picks, that statement is completely true and is not considered libel or slander. Bear in mind that this is not intended as official law advice and every country, state and province has different laws. Be sure to check the laws in your area before mentioning anyone's name in one of your advertisements.

Another good way to use examples is to mention TV shows or New Programs that they've appeared on. This is used extensively to sell poorly reviewed products. For instance, a particularly low-quality keyboard may have been reviewed in a popular musician's magazine. Even if the magazine rated the keyboard very low and gave it a bad review, you can still use a phrase like "Featured in Piano&Synth Magazine!" Once again this is technically true, the product was, in fact, featured in the magazine. There's no need to mention that it was panned by reviewers or got a low score, just use the exposure to sell the product. This goes back to the old adage, "No publicity is bad publicity."

Keywords are Killer!

Using appropriate keywords is one of the best ways to get your ads noticed. The one downfall of Craigslist is that the ads are so temporary that it's highly unlikely for you to get any results in major search engines like Google or Yahoo!. Luckily you don't need to; you can still get all the exposure you need through Craigslist using its own search engine.

One method that many people use is to put random, popular keywords at the bottom of their posting. This has limited success. On one hand you are slightly more likely to get off beat clicks from people looking for completely unrelated products and services. That's about the only upside though. People looking for different products and services probably aren't interested in what you've posted about anyway and people who are interested are almost always put off by seeing a big stack of generic keywords at the bottom of your post. It makes your post seem like a possible scam.

The best practice is to use related keywords where they actually make sense. Instead of just listing keywords randomly at the bottom of your post, you can try to implement them where they actually make sense within your ad. It also helps to read through your ad and see if there are any generic terms you can turn into specific keywords or specific phrases you can turn into generic keywords.

If you're offering service as a computer repairman then instead of saying "I can work on any computer" you can say "Proficient in PC and MAC using Windows, OSX and Linux." We've lost some of our brevity but we've gained some important keywords: PC, Mac, OSX, Windows and Linux. People might have a specific need for one of those computers or operating systems and your ad only says that you can work on "any computer" they might not find you! Now you'll be getting hits from people who have all three operating systems and need help.

Placement of keywords is also important. Titles are the number 1 marketable part of your ad. A bad title can turn the most beautifully written advertisement into a complete waste of time. If no one is interested in your ad then you won't get any clicks or exposure. And, as I've mentioned, people tend to search within titles only to avoid keyword bombing (When people put unrelated keywords in their postings). It's very important to put relevant keywords in your ad title that will attract clients in customers. Using our example above you might change this title: "Computer Repairman, I'll work on any computer!" to "Windows, OSX and Linux Computer Technician." By adding the keywords in your title you've greatly expanded the amount of people who will find your ad via searching.

One of the best ways to think of good keywords is to actually search Craigslist for something that more or less matches what you're trying to post. Take note of the top results and see what kind of keywords and titles they used. Try not to copy from them directly but definitely learn from what they did and use it to your advantage. You could combined the keyword usage of the top 5 entries and you'll have a single entry that's better than any one of theirs.

Organize Your Listing

We've already discussed that people don't like to read giant blocks of text or sift through shaky grammar. Another pet peeve of potential clients is trying to find relevant information. People look for certain details when they go to buy a product or seek out a service.

If you're selling a computer, you shouldn't write the specifications somewhere within your advertisements in paragraph style. People seeking computers want to immediately know the computer specifications and often if it takes them more than 2 seconds to find the specifications they'll just move on to another ad. Computers and most other electronic devices should have their specifications written clearly at the top in a tabular manner like so:

Computer: Dell OptiPlex 755
Processor: Intel Core 2 Duo 2.33GHz
RAM: 6GB DDR2 PC-6400
Video Card: ATI Radeon HD 4670
Keyboard: Included (HP 108-key)
Mouse: Not Included

This allows the potential customer to skim through the pertinent information and stay on the page longer. Here's another example:

Car: 1991 Honda Accord
Color: Blue Green
Engine: 2.1 Liter V4
Mileage: 230,000 Miles
Gas Mileage: 20MPG City, 24MPG Highway
Title: Pink Slip In Hand, passed smog
Condition: Good
Kelly Blue Book Value: $1,800

By putting the absolutely pertinent information at the top you allow the client to get interested in the product and remain on the page. This can be a double-edged blade. If your item is not in like-new condition then this set up might allow the potential client to spot the flaw and move on fast.

Sometimes it helps to burry less-than-stellar information within the rest of your post. Again, this seems sneaky, but we're not trying to swindle anyone we're just piquing their interest. The point of advertising online in this way is to get people interested in buying the product, the rest of the sales magic usually happens when the customer comes to review the product in person.

It's always a good idea to disclose important information about non-functioning and/or broken items to avoid unhappy customers and potential lawsuits, but when you disclose that information is up to you, as long as it's BEFORE the customer has paid you or signed any type of contract. The customer deserves a chance to back out of the deal if he or she feels that the product or service isn't what he or she ultimately wants.

A customer will likely forgive you for waiting 'till the last minute to mention a shortcoming of the product but finding out about problems in products only after already buying them will result in very angry, ex-customers. It's just bad for business. In general you should try to be as honest as possible about what you're selling or providing and if there are problems with the product or service, downplaying product flaws is preferred over omission.

3. Sell Your Junk!

Craigslist is commonly known as the world's largest virtual garage sale. Just about anything you imagine can be put up for sale. In that respect it's essentially a digital classifieds paper of massive proportions.

Simply getting rid of unwanted items or trading unused items for necessities is one of the most basic ways of turning a profit on Craigslist. You do have to be careful about what you post though. Some items are restricted from being posted on craigslist.

What you can and cannot sell

Craigslist isn't particularly strict on enforcing its policies. This is because there are so many millions of listings being posted every day that it would be nearly impossible to moderate without automated software.

That being said, they take the safety of their users and cooperation with law enforcement very seriously. The following items are prohibited from being offered for sale on Craigslist.org. You may see listings for some of these items anyway but my advice is to stay clear.

Obscene Material: This is for legal (and arguably moral) reasons. Any type of illegal adult content (especially child pornography) is strictly prohibited from being posted.

Weapons etc.: This includes firearms, disguised/switchable knives, martial arts weapons, scopes, silencers, ammo, magazines, BB guns, pellet guns, tear gas or stun guns (among other things.

Fireworks & Explosives: No fireworks or explosive materials of any kind are permitted to be posted (regardless of safety).

Illegal Drugs & Controlled Substances: This includes drug paraphernalia.

Alcohol or Tobacco: No alcoholic drinks, smokable or non-smokable tobacco products are allowed.

Prescription Drugs & Medical Devices: This includes prescription contact lenses, defibrillators, hypodermic needles and hearing aids.

Blood, Bodily Fluids or Body Parts: This is self explanatory. If you plan on selling any of these on a classified-style website please put the book down and seek counsel.

Pets of any kind: This is specifically in regards to *selling* pets. It's okay to adopt out pets even if there's a small adoption fee. I don't recommend using Craigslist as a resource for adopting pets, however.

Pesticides: or hazardous substances, or items containing hazardous substances including but not limited to contaminated toys, or art or craft material containing toxic substances without a warning label.

Illegal telecommunications equipment: including but not limited to access cards, password sniffers, access card programmers and "unloopers", or cable descramblers

Stolen property: or property with serial number removed or altered.

Burglary tools: including but not limited to lock-picks or motor vehicle master keys

False identification cards: items with police insignia, citizenship documents, or birth certificates.

Counterfeit currency: coins and stamps, tickets, as well as equipment designed to make them.

Counterfeit: replica or knock-off brand name goods.

Material that infringes copyright: including but not limited to software or other digital goods you are not authorized to sell, warez, bootlegs (without consent of the band).

Airline tickets: that restrict transfer, and tickets of any kind which you are not authorized to sell.

Coupons: or gift cards that restrict transfer, and coupons or gift cards which you are not authorized to sell.

Gambling items: including but not limited to lottery tickets, sports trading card 'grab bags', raffle tickets, sweepstakes entries or slot machines.

Used or rebuilt batteries: or batteries containing mercury.

Used bedding and clothing: unless sanitized in accordance with law.

Non-packaged food items: or adulterated food.

Bulk email: or mailing lists that contain names, addresses, phone numbers, or other personal identifying information

Aside from those major things to avoid you can pretty much sell anything. Popular items include: video game systems, computers, computer components, cars, auto parts, trading cards, antiques, furniture, cell phones, toys, bicycles, event tickets and CD's/DVD's.

How to Market Your Items

Being able to market your unwanted items is the key to being able to sell them to strangers on craigslist. A poorly written or uninformative ad will not get you any sales and nothing drives potential customers away faster than annoying ads!

Just because you're selling your own personal items in garage-sale fashion doesn't mean you have to be unprofessional about it. Using professional-sounding marketing lingo and commercial advertising tactics works just as well on craigslist as just about any other medium.

Using Advertising Language to Market

It's a good idea to develop a paradigm for how you present your items for sale on Craigslist. Make a template that pretty much stays the same and then fill in the blanks for each individual item. This allows you to have consistency so when people see more and more of your listings they will come to recognize you. Building a rapport with your potential customer base is essential to repeat success.

You should also be aware of how you describe your goods. Look up your products at other online retailers and see how they're marketing. Use key phrases that are associated with your product and point out specific features that are noteworthy.

Your message should be reassuring and hype-building. The viewer needs to be intrigued and convinced that they need your item for one reason or another. For example: If you're selling a professional-grade camera then don't just list it's specifications, tell the potential buyer what he or she can use the camera for and how it's superior to its competitors. Just remember to consider the "keep it brief" rule while you're writing your ads. Short, powerful sentences are best. Bullet points and lists of examples or features are also a great tool as they combined thorough explanation of the product with the brevity required to keep peoples' attention.

Combos, Bonuses and Best Offers, Oh My!

Another thing you see a lot of in professional advertisements is the inclusion of special offers. This is effective as it reassures the customer that, not only are they getting their money's worth, but they're getting a great deal as well. On Craigslist this can be as simple as selling a lot of items combined instead of individually.

Let's say you're selling a popular video game console and you're also looking to sell the individual games as well. You can put all of them on a single sales page. Offer the console and the games separately at whatever prices you choose and then, at the end of your ad, offer them all together with slight discount to the overall price as a bonus for buying the whole lot. (E.G. Sell the console for $100, the games for $20 and if the viewer buys the console and 3 games it only costs $140 instead of $160.)

Another thing to remember is that these ads are time sensitive and you can always get rid of your ad when the item is sold, modify it if conditions are changed or delete and re-post it to get a fresh start. A good tactic is to add time-sensitive bonuses. Offer to cut 20% off the price if the buyer responds by the end of the day. Alternatively you can do the opposite. If you're trying to market a popular or hard-to-sell item then it may be a good idea to start a little high and gradually reduce the price if no one has made an offer.

The last thing to remember about special offers is this simple little abbreviation: *O.B.O.* It stands for "Or Best Offer." This is very common in the cars/trucks section of craigslist as people are generally more likely to haggle on car prices then other items. Sometimes mentioning that you're willing to haggle can be the difference between getting a bite or not. If you're willing to accept a little less then it doesn't hurt to mention it but if you do, expect to be almost definitely offered a little less (hence it's good to start higher than you think the item is worth). If you're not willing to negotiate on the price and you don't need to sell the item fast, you can use the keyword *firm*.

To Sell, or to Toss? That is the Question.

Nobody likes to admit that some of their favorite "treasures" are only special to them and them alone. Some items just aren't going to sell anytime soon either because they're personal items that other people are put off by or they're obsolete items that aren't appreciating in value.

If you're going to be posting a lot of ads on Craigslist then it's important to consider whether or not the items you're selling are actually going to turn a profit or if you should just toss them. Being a packrat can be a great starting point for amassing a collection of merchandise to sell but it can also be your downfall if you don't understand the value of what you have. It's also pertinent to consider when and where you're trying to sell your goods as these factors play a major role in who's buying from you. It doesn't hurt to list these items, you might get a hit. But ultimately you have to decide if it's worth your time to post an ad with a near-zero percent chance of success. As they say, time is money.

Obsolete & Out of Sight

Some of the hardest to sell items in the world are old electronics and utilitarian devices that have become obsolete. Very few of these things gain value until they become extremely old. Sure, there are exceptions. Anything that was rare, limited or the first of its kind has a good chance of being valuable. Most of these items were valuable when they first appeared though. Anything that was ubiquitous or widespread when it first came out probably hasn't gained much value.

Old computers are probably the hardest sell as they often have little-to-no value to today's potential customers. If you have a home PC from between 1987 and 1999 it's very unlikely that you're going to sell it easily because even the strongest and most expensive computers from those times don't even come close to the economy/low-expense computers that are available today. Even a $1,000 computer from 2000 has less than 15% the power of a $500 computer from today's market. Unless your old PC (or MAC) is a known collectible or rare find, you're better of recycling it. This also applies to old computer accessories like floppy discs and zip drives.

This doesn't just apply to personal computers. Just about any communications device from the past 20 or 30 years is of limited value. Old cell phones aren't even usable today, pagers have been obsolete for years and even corded telephones are scarce these days. Even if you find buyers for some of these items, remember that this is generally an in-person pick up situation. How much money will you really get for a single corded telephone that's 10 years old? Will that be worth your time and gas money, or the customers?

One exception to the electronics rule is the video game console. Most of the time these are considered collectible and regardless of what time period they're in they can still be useful because they're entertainment devices and not utilitarian objects. Keep in mind the same cannot be said for cassette tapes, video cassettes, beta cassettes, laser discs and 8-tracks. Despite the entertainment value of those devices they're generally not held in as high of esteem as game consoles and only the rare and collectible will turn a profit.

The last thing to remember about obsolete products is software. Computer software that's more than 10 years old is very likely to be obsolete and of limited value. These might be worth trying to sell if you have a large collection and plan on selling the entire thing. Not all customers have a concept of what software is relevant or up-to-date so there is some leeway here. If you can convince the customer that there is a big deal to be had and lots of content, you might get away with selling obsolete software. Just make sure it's at least compatible with modern computer technology.

Family Treasures

Junior's macaroni Picasso might look great on the fridge but it's probably not going to draw in a lot of customers, at least not the kind you want to meet in person and do business with. Some items are best left in the family or, if there's no other choice, thrown away. Homemade items do have a place on craigslist but you have to remember that not everyone's idea of quality is exactly the same.

Engraved sports trophies, homemade art projects and used school supplies aren't exactly at the top of the "hot items" list when it comes to selling things online. If there's a small market for these types of nostalgic treasures it's decidedly small and of questionable value. Old toys and used personal items might be sellable but consider the condition they're in and how useful they might be to a potential buyer. If you're selling these types of items just to get rid of them then you might consider just throwing them out or stuffing them in a shed instead.

Is it Seasonal? Timing is Key

How often do you decide to go out and buy a new winter coat? Is it something you're considering during the sweltering summer? What about bathing suits and sandals, notice any good deals on those types of items during the harsh winter? Some items are seasonal and really don't make sense to try and sell at the wrong time. Even if you do get a buyer they might expect a much lower than normal price because it's off season.

Fall & Winter: Coats, gloves, pants, fur boots, pajamas, heaters, firewood, umbrellas, ponchos, blankets and (In the Northern Hemisphere) Holiday Decorations are items that tend to be popular during the cold autumn and winter months but aren't particularly popular during summer as they aren't really needed. Popular items also sell very well during the gift-giving holidays (winter in the north, summer in the south) so it may be pertinent to wait until those holidays come close to sell heavily popular and hard-to-obtain items as they will fetch a higher price. Pets will also have an advantage if adopted in the winter because the spring population boom will saturate the market and make them harder to place.

Spring & Summer: Bathing suits, sandals, sunglasses, fans, coolers, shorts, tank-tops, sunscreen, tanning lotion, bottled water, sporting equipment, school supplies, flower/grass seed, swimming pools, gardening equipment and construction tools tend to sell more during the summer than the winter (again for utilization reasons).

Safety Tips for In-Person Exchanges

Craigslist is a wonderful tool for advertising, marketing, communication and networking but it has it's pitfalls as well. One of the weaknesses of selling items on Craigslist is that you will generally be expected to meet people in person to trade the items for money etc.

Unless the item is something extremely large it is recommended to meet the person in a public place like a diner or café. If you're meeting this person for the first time it is a good idea to bring a friend with you. When meeting someone in person cash is always preferable. Avoid taking checks, money orders or anything that can't be verified right away. If the customer is willing to pay in advance, PayPal is a safe and acceptable form of payment.

4. Selling Digital Content

Craigslist is not limited to physical items. You can just as easily use Craigslist as an advertising platform for your online store. Selling digital downloads is easy and very cost effective. Generally speaking it's a lot cheaper to pay for the bandwidth to download content than to write it to a physical medium and produce it.

Ideas for Products

E-Tutorials are popular items on the web. These can be in the form of pay-membership websites, e-books, video courses, audio MP3 courses or slide shows. There are a variety of tools you can use to create instructional content on everything from Internet marketing to baking a cake from scratch.

If you're a musical artist or know a local group that you can manage you can use Craigslist as a way of distributing your music for pay. This is a lot cheaper than creating demo CD's and actually has more potential for developing a fan base since people will find your music by searching on the internet instead of just word of mouth.

Methods of Distribution

Craigslist is a great way to advertise your digital items but there are no built-in tools for distributing them. Your best bet is to have a separate website with an online shopping cart. Craigslist will get the people to your website and it will do the rest. You can find a lot of specific information on using custom shopping carts just by searching for them on your favorite search engine. PayPal is especially recommended as they are a trusted website and provide explicit instructions.

If you don't want to hassle with trying to figure out how to implement an online shopping cart you can uses a well-known online retailer like www.Ebay.com, www.Etsy.com or www.cafepress.com. These sellers sometimes charge a fee for putting an item up for sell or require a monthly/yearly membership. The benefit is that they do almost all the work for you. The online shopping cart and web interface is complete controlled by the website and you just get to stick around for the profits. A lot of these websites act like search engines so they have a lot of the same functionality as Craigslist. The difference is that Craigslist has a massive user base and a 15-year reputation to back it up.

Copyright Info and Things to Watch Out For

One caveat to selling anything online is that you're publicly displaying your content for the world to see. Any material that's offensive or potentially infringes on someone's rights (whether you realize it or not) has a much higher chance of being seen and acted upon.

Every country has specific copyright laws but let's focus on the U.S. copyright laws because they're some of the most extensive rights laws of any country. According to the U.S. Copyright Law, using content created by another party without that party's consent is infringing on their copy rights. This is especially dangerous if you're profiting off the material as you could have to pay the original artist back in potentially lost revenue. If you're not sure where an image, a textual excerpt, an audio sample or a video file have come from, it's generally a good idea not to use them in your online content.

The DMCA (Digital Millennium Copyright Act) is another U.S. law that specifically prohibits distribution of certain types of digital content and provides provisions regarding rights to digital works. These are generally the same as the U.S. Copyright Law. One thing to watch out for is that the DMCA prohibits distribution of any software that is designed to circumvent or bypass copy-protection software built into many of today's modern mediums.

A PC video game is a good example. It would be illegal and a very bad idea to make digital copies of a popular computer game with a "cracking" program to bypass the game's activation so that you could sell them for cheap online. Copying the game in order to distribute it violates the U.S. Copyright law and bypassing the game's anti-piracy software violates the DMCA.

It is, however, legal to sell your physical copy of the PC video game to another person along with any information they need to legally activate and register the software. This is legal because you're not making a copy for someone else and retaining one for yourself; you're transferring property from yourself to another person. The same goes for music CD's, Computer software, Movies and books.

Because there really isn't an effective way of controlling how many people download content or proving that you haven't retained a copy it's not advised to try and sell any type of copyrighted content via download.

It's also important to remember that you may be taxed on certain items that you sell. This varies widely by area and, truth be told, we could write a whole 50-page book on different state and country ordinances alone. Be sure to research your local laws and find out whether or not you'll have to worry about paying taxes on income you've made selling items online. Generally most people don't think about it when they're trading used items for cash but selling digital downloads online makes it a pretty hard issue to avoid.

5. Sell Your Services

Using Craigslist as a virtual storefront is only one of many, many different ways you can get the service to make you money. Offering your own services is a great way to get freelance-style contract work and earn extra cash. There's a lot of money to be made in service fields like computer repair and tutoring.

What You Can and Cannot Offer

Obviously there are some services that you are not allowed to offer on the Craigslist website:

(1) Prostitution: This sort of goes without saying but you'd be surprised how many people post listings for it anyway. This is dependent on your state and federal government's laws but is generally frowned upon by the people of Craigslist.
(2) Bullying/Violence: This seems silly as well but it's not lawful to advertise any service that promotes violence. A bodyguard service would be okay but advertising that you'll beat up other people is not.
(3) Illegal Services: Dealing drugs, buying alcohol for minors, theft, scamming or any other illegal activity is prohibited.

The main types of services people offer are in repair and general freelance work.

Popular Areas of Service

Here are some popular, lucrative areas of service you can post advertisements for:

Computer: Repairing and servicing computers is one of the most popular service categories on craigslist. If you're good with computers you should definitely try this one out. Millions of people have computer problems every day and a great deal of them would prefer to pay a local person to come fix their computer than get charged ridiculous amounts of money at a big chain computer retailer.

Creative: This is another big category. With this you can do just about anything art related such as: creating business cards, designing tattoos, building web pages, doing album artwork, photographic events, writing speeches and videotaping weddings. The creative category is very broad and encompasses a lot of different skills that people need every day.

Lessons: This category is used extensively by people who can't afford high-priced tutoring centers. Those well-known institutions can charge people as much as $3,000 per semester! If you've completed highs school or any amount of college you should have no problem helping kids in the K-8 grades with homework etc. This category is also a good place to find adult tutees who are seeking training in computer programs or refresher courses in college subjects like math and English.

Pet: People love to take care of their pets but paying $250 to get Fluffy's hair trimmed and claws painted is usually out of most people's budgets. If you have any experience taking care of animals or grooming them, this can be an extremely lucrative category for you. You can charge half the price of a local dog or cat groomer and still turn a hefty profit because the number one resources required for pet care are time and patience.

Automotive: Garages and mechanics charging people too much is even more ubiquitous than overpriced pet care. A lot of people know how to fix cars but have no desire to be mechanics professionally. If you're one of those people who just has a penchant for replacing radiators and silencing squeaky belts then this is the category for you. Car repair isn't the only thing you can offer. If you have equipment for custom paint jobs or if you own a transportation vehicle like a bus or limousine then this is where you'll want to advertise for yourself as well.

Farm + Garden: This can be a difficult category to get hits on but only because it's absolutely flooded with qualified people posting advertisements. After all, it's not exactly rocket science to be able to pick up basic gardening tools and work on beautifying people's yards. Despite how rudimentary yard work really is, you'd be surprised how many people are just unwilling to do it themselves and would rather pay someone else to pull their weeds.

Household: This is sort of a generic, house-related category. Anything from plumbing and carpentry to carpet cleaning and maid service can be found on this page. This is also where you'll want to post if you're looking to be a babysitter or a nanny. Weather conditioning and cooler repair also fit into this category.

Skilled Trade: This is a more specific category where you'll want to post if you are a professional or have a lot of experience in a particular trade. This could include things like: Carpentry, Plumbing, Electrical, Masonry, Furniture Making, Painting or Tile Installation.

Writing/Editing/Translation: This is an extremely useful place to post and look for services. If you know how to speak more than one language you can post advertisements for translation services; people generally prefer human translations because they tend to be more accurate and less formal and automated. If you're a decent writer or editor you can consult people on their writing assignments or offer to write résumés or college admission letters.

How to Market Yourself

When your posting an advertisement about a service you'll perform it's important to remember that you're essentially selling yourself. You can make up your own template but a good format to start with is one as follows:

1. Service to be provided

2. Relevant experience in subject area.

3. Examples of Work (Links or images)

4. Contact information and instructions.

The first thing you should mention briefly is what service you're providing. It should be short and concise. Remember from earlier sections that it's important to use keywords in your titles. Consider the following examples:

Mediocre title: "Got a leak? I can fix any sink and patch any pipe!"

Effective Title: "Experienced Plumber: I can fix any sink & repair any pipe"

The second title is more effective because it uses more key words (plumber, experienced, fix, sink, repair) than the original title. More people are likely to find this post because the title describes what they are looking for.

The next thing to worry about is what experience you have. It's pertinent to mention how many years you've used this particular skill and whether or not you have a degree or certificate in the field.

If it's applicable you should provide people with examples of your work. This can be a link to an external website that features your work or just pictures that you upload to Craigslist.

Lastly you should provide your contact information. In a résumé it's important to have the contact information at the top but this is an internet sales ad and they're read completely differently.

Avoid putting your full address or cell phone number in your contact information. It's probably best to just leave your business e-mail and it's completely acceptable to use the anonymized e-mail that Craigslist provides; just mention that so people know they can reach you that way.

6. To Conclude...

As you've seen there is a ton of money to be made in various outlets of Craigslist. It would be easy to write a book two or three times the length of this one on all the different ins and outs of Craigslist.org; it's a very complex site despite how easy it is to use.

One thing you should keep with you is that Craigslist is a two-way street. You can use any of these examples on how to make money and reverse them for examples on how to get good deals. Anywhere you post an ad for your item or service there's equal opportunity to post an ad seeking a particular item or service. Saving money is just another form of making money so getting great deals on Craigslist is another effective way to profit from this spectacular website.

You've been briefed and given enough information to turn Craigslist.org into your own personal treasure trove. All that's left is for you to take the initiative to get out there and sell, sell, sell! (Or buy, buy, buy if that's your angle.) Have fun and explore, there are plenty of Craigslist secrets yet to be uncovered!

www.ingramcontent.com/pod-product-compliance
Lightning Source LLC
LaVergne TN
LVHW021345200726
843509LV00014B/2685